My Rhyme Time

Old MaCdohald had a Farm

and other singing rhymes

Miles Kelly

Little Bo-peep

Little Bo-peep has lost her sheep
And doesn't know where to find them.
Leave them alone and they'll come home,
Bringing their tails behind them.

Jack and Jill

Jack and Jill went up the hill
To fetch a pail of water.
Jack fell down and broke his crown
And Jill came tumbling after.

Up Jack got and home did trot
As fast as he could caper.
He went to bed to mend his head
With vinegar and brown paper.

Sing a Song of Sixpence

Sing a song of sixpence,

A pocket full of rye.

Four and twenty blackbirds,

Baked in a pie.

When the pie was opened,

The birds began to sing;

Wasn't that a dainty dish,

To set before the king?

The king was in his counting house,
Counting out his money;
The queen was in the parlour,
Eating bread and honey.

The maid was in the garden,
Hanging out the clothes;
When down came a blackbird
And pecked off her nose!

Three Blind Mice

Three blind mice,
three blind mice,
See how they run, see how they run!
They all ran after the farmer's Wife,
Who cut off their tails with a carving Knife,
Did you ever see such a thing in your life,
As three blind mice?

Humpty Dumpty

Humpty Dumpty sat on a wall,
Humpty Dumpty had a great fall
All the king's horses and all the king's men
Couldn't put Humpty together again.

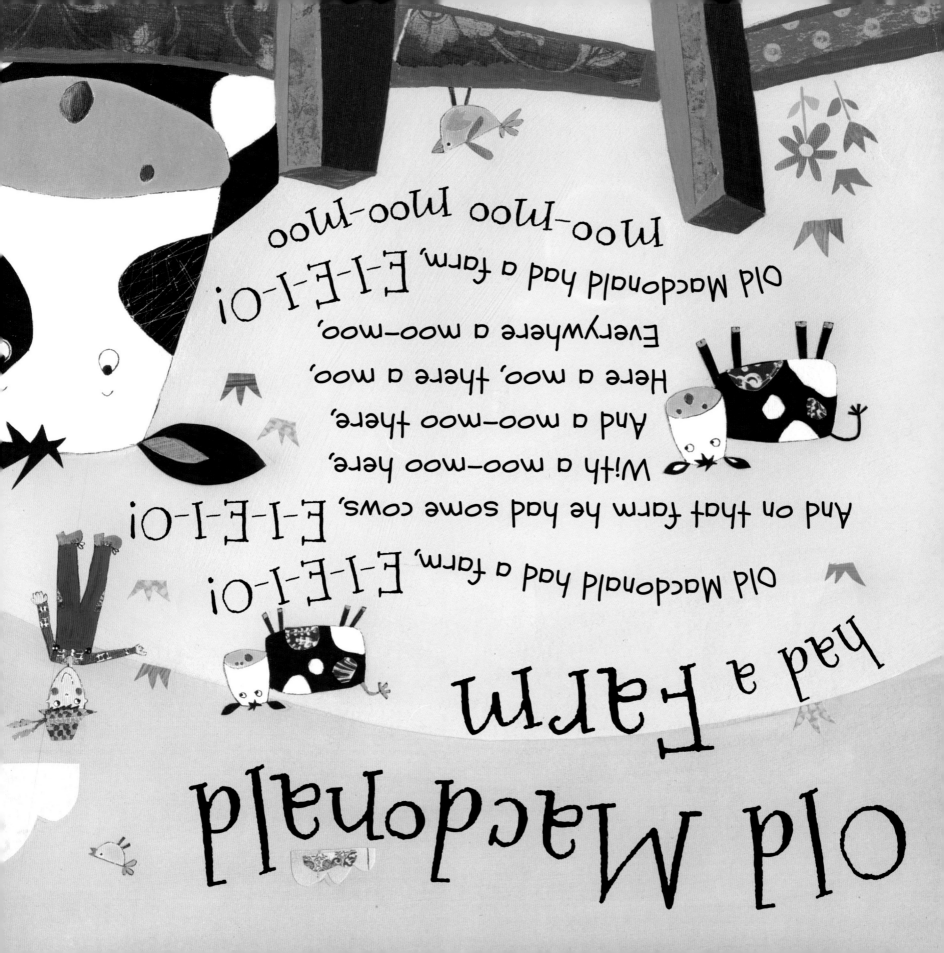

Old Macdonald had a Farm

Old Macdonald had a farm, E-I-E-I-O!
And on that farm he had some cows, E-I-E-I-O!
With a moo-moo here,
And a moo-moo there,
Here a moo, there a moo,
Everywhere a moo-moo.
Old Macdonald had a farm, E-I-E-I-O!
Moo-moo moo-moo moo

Old Macdonald had a farm, E-I-E-I-O!
And on that farm he had some sheep, E-I-E-I-O!
With a baa-baa here,
And a baa-baa there,
Here a baa, there a baa,
everywhere a baa-baa,
Old Macdonald had a farm, E-I-E-I-O!

baa-baa
baa-baa

Old Macdonald had a farm, E-I-E-I-O!
And on that farm he had some ducks, E-I-E-I-O!
With a quack-quack here,
And a quack-quack there,
Here a quack, there a quack,
everywhere a quack-quack,
Old Macdonald had a farm, E-I-E-I-O!

quack-quack
quack-quack

oink-oink
oink-oink

Old Macdonald had a farm, E-I-E-I-O!

And on that farm he had some pigs, E-I-E-I-O!
With an oink-oink here,
And an oink-oink there,
Here an oink, there an oink,
everywhere an oink-oink,
Old Macdonald had a farm, E-I-E-I-O!

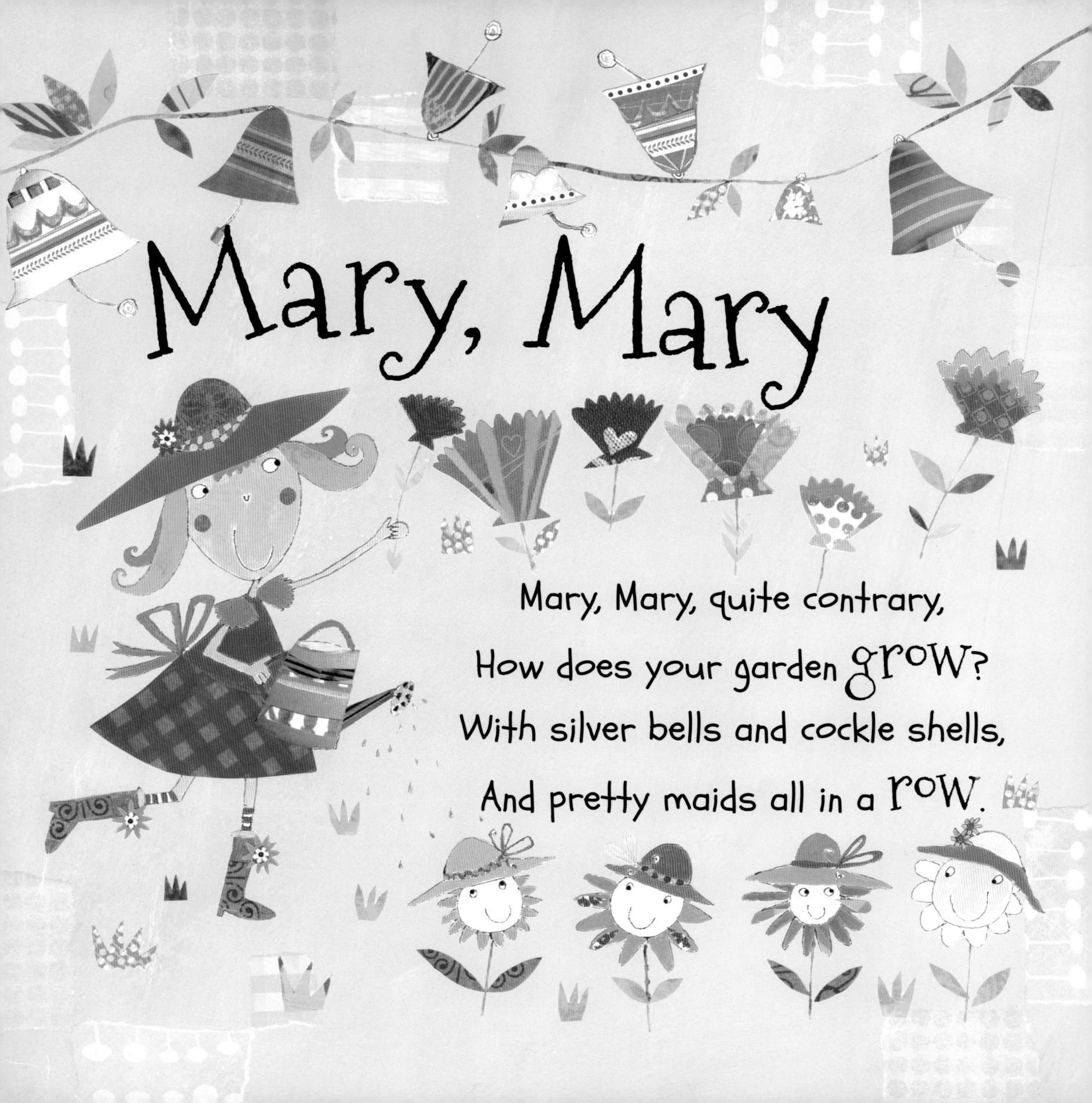

Mary, Mary

Mary, Mary, quite contrary,

How does your garden grow?

With silver bells and cockle shells,

And pretty maids all in a row.

Baa, Baa, Black Sheep

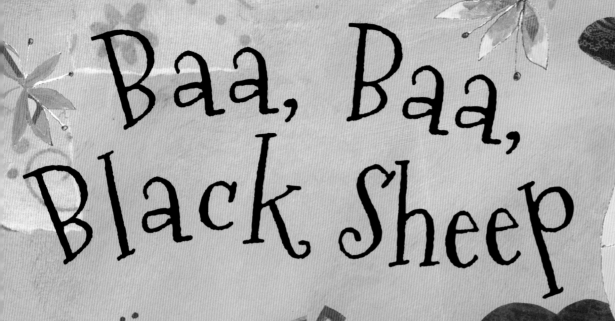

Baa, baa, black sheep,
Have you any wool?
Yes, sir, yes, sir,
Three bags full.
One for the master,
One for the dame,
And one for the little boy
Who lives down the lane.

Girls and Boys Come Out to Play

Girls and boys come out to play,
The moon does shine as bright as day.
Leave your supper, and leave your sleep,
And come with your playfellows into the street.

Come with a whoop, come with a call,
Come with a good will or not at all.
Up the ladder and down the wall,
A halfpenny loaf will serve us all.
You find milk, and I'll find flour,
And we'll have a pudding in half an hour.

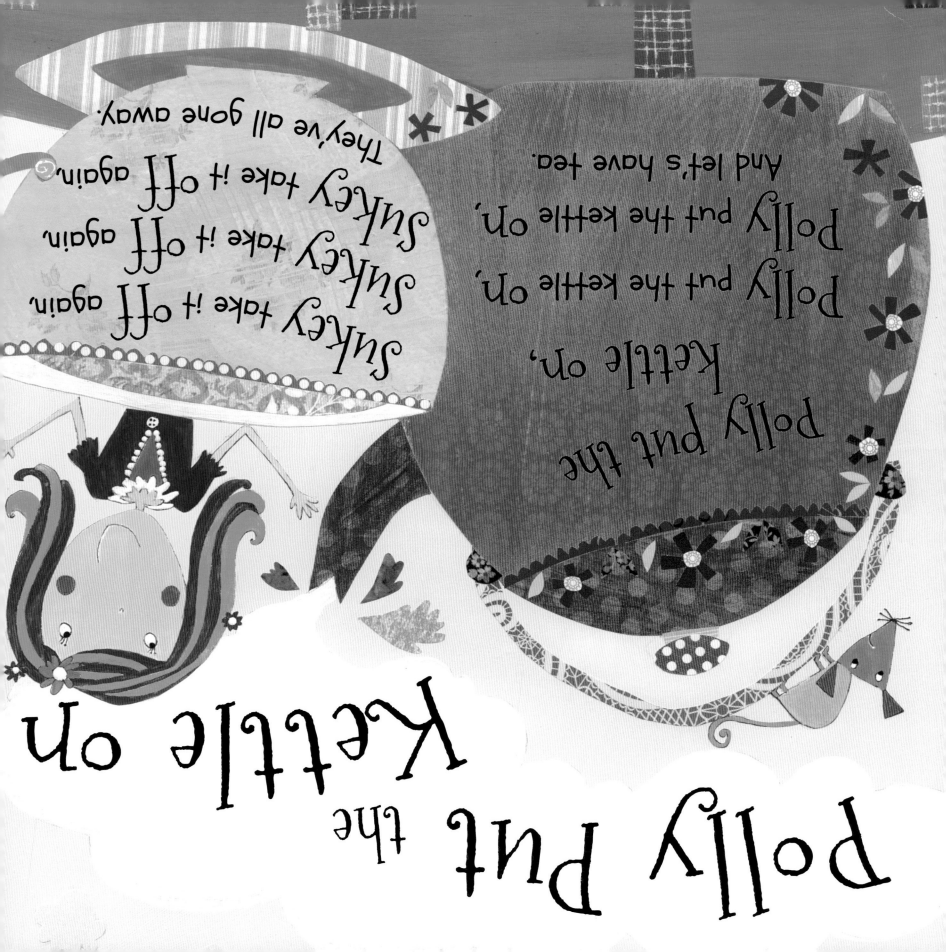

Polly put the
kettle on,
Polly put the kettle on,
Polly put the kettle on,
And let's have tea.

Sukey take it off again,
Sukey take it off again,
Sukey take it off again,
They've all gone away.

Polly Put the Kettle on

Little Miss Muffet

Little Miss Muffet
sat on a tuffet
Eating her curds and whey,
Along came a spider,
Who sat down beside her
And frightened Miss Muffet away.

The Wheels on the Bus

The wheels on the bus go
round and round,
Round and round,
round and round.
The wheels on the bus go
round and round,
All day long.

The horn on the bus goes
Beep, beep, beep,
Beep, beep, beep,
Beep, beep, beep.
The horn on the bus goes
Beep, beep, beep,
All day long.

The windscreen wipers go
Swish, swish, swish,
Swish, swish, swish,
Swish, swish, swish,
The windscreen wipers go
Swish, swish, swish,
All day long.

The people on the bus bounce
up and down,
Up and down, up and down.
The people on the bus bounce
up and down,
All day long.

The daddies on the bus go
nod, nod, nod,
Nod, nod, nod, nod, nod, nod.
The daddies on the bus go
nod, nod, nod,
All day long.

The mummies on the bus go
chatter, chatter, chatter,
Chatter, chatter, chatter,
chatter, chatter, chatter.
The mummies on the bus go
chatter, chatter, chatter,
All day long.

Pease Porridge Hot

Pease porridge hot,
Pease porridge cold,
Pease porridge in the pot
Nine days old.

Some like it hot,
Some like it cold,
Some like it in the pot

Nine days old!

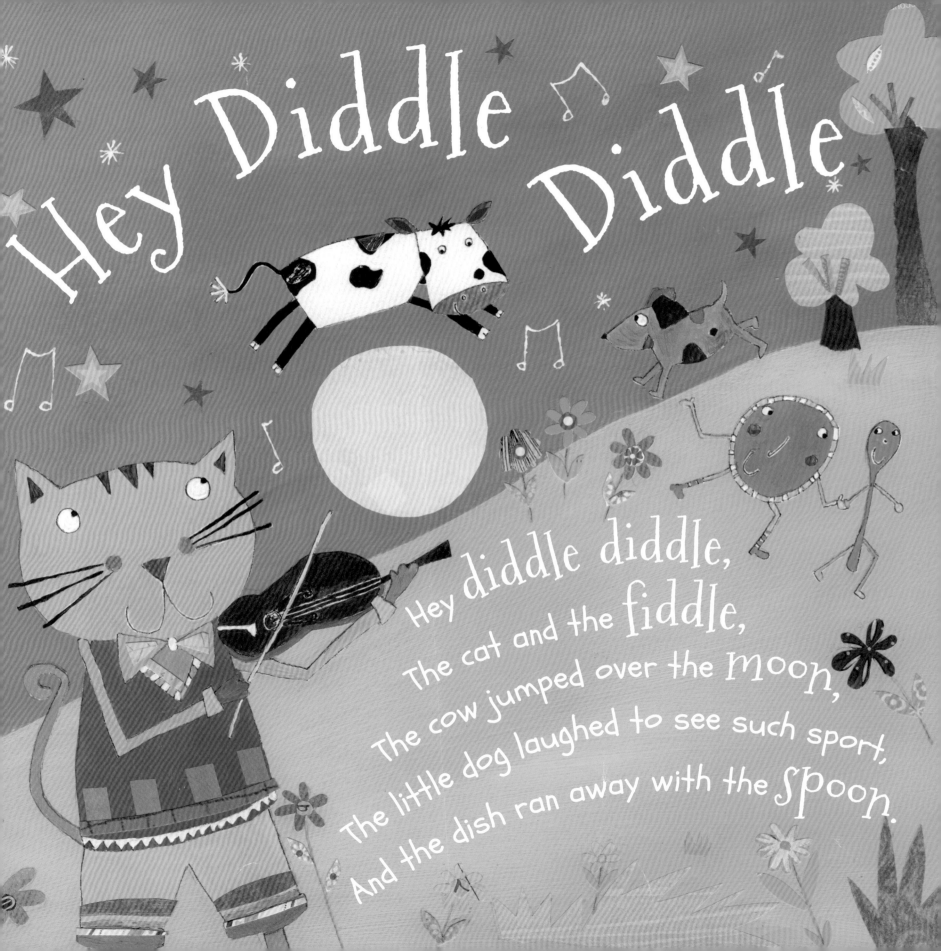

Hey Diddle Diddle

Hey diddle diddle,
The cat and the fiddle,
The cow jumped over the moon,
The little dog laughed to see such sport,
And the dish ran away with the spoon.

The End

My Rhyme Time

Old MaCdohald had a Farm
and other singing rhymes

Time to sing! Little ones will love sharing and singing these familiar rhymes every day. Favourite characters are beautifully illustrated on every page, making this a book to treasure.

Illustrated by The Pope Twins

Miles Kelly
www.mileskelly.net

Printed in China
Mfg date: Jun 2016
Batch number: SRT316

ISBN 978-1-78209-438-8

9 781782 094388

UK £5.99/US $7.95 RRP

KR-934-724